It's fun to draw™ Cars, Planes and Trains

Mark Bergin

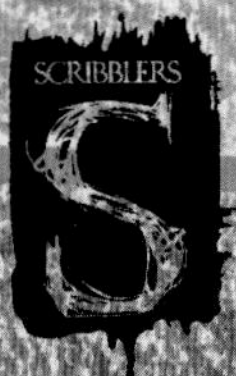

Author:
Mark Bergin was born in Hastings, England. He has illustrated an award winning series and written over twenty books. His work includes book designs layouts and storyboards in many styles including cartoon for numerous books, posters and adverts. He lives in Bexhill-on-sea with his wife and three children.

Editorial Assistant:
Rob Walker

HOW TO USE THIS BOOK:
Start by following the numbered splats on the left hand page. These steps will ask you to add some lines to your drawing. The new lines are always drawn in red so you can see how the drawing builds from step to step. The 'You can do it!' splats suggest the best drawing and colouring techniques to use.

Published in Great Britain in MMXV by
Scribblers, a division of Book House
25 Marlborough Place, Brighton BN1 1UB
www.salariya.com
www.book-house.co.uk

ISBN-13: 978-1-910184-22-6

1 3 5 7 9 8 6 4 2

A CIP catalogue record for this book is available from the British Library.

Printed and bound in China.

Contents

Sports car

1 Start with the main body of the car.

2 Add the wheels and a line for the ground.

Splat-a-fact
Sports cars have very fast acceleration.

You can do it!
Use a felt-tip for the lines. Add highlights with wax crayon then brush ink colour over it.

3 Draw in the roof and the windows.

4 Add the driver and a spoiler at the back of the car.

5 Add finishing details.

Aerobatic plane

1 Start by drawing the plane's fuselage (body).

2 Draw in the canopy and tail fin.

You can do it!

Use a felt-tip for the lines and add colour using coloured pencils.

Splat-a-fact

Aerobatic planes perform acrobatic manoeuvres in formation.

3 Draw in the wings.

4 Add the pilot and tail fin number.

5 Add finishing details and motion lines.

Steam locomotive

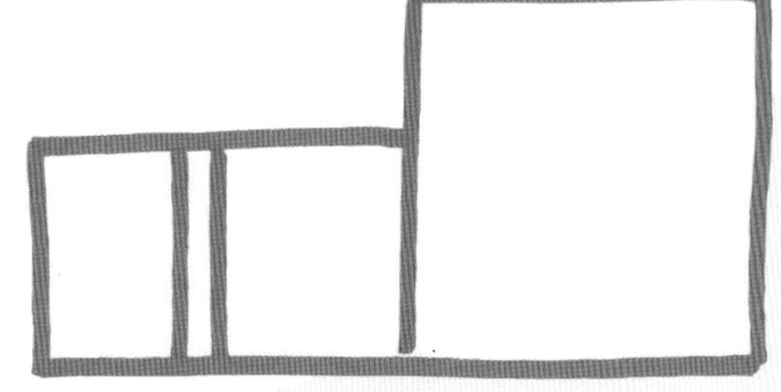

1 Start by drawing the main body of the locomotive.

You can do it!

Use a felt-tip for the lines. Use coloured oil pastels to add colour.

2 Add the chimney, dome and roof.

3 Draw in the wheels. Add lines for the railway track.

4 Add the driver and the finishing details.

Splat-a-fact

Steam power drives the locomotives wheels.

Learjet

1 Draw the jet's fuselage with a big black dot for the nose.

2 Draw in the windscreen.

3 Draw in the twin jet engines.

You can do it!

Use a felt-tip for the lines. Use wax crayon for detail then paint on top, the wax will act as a resistant.

4 Draw in the wings.

Splat-a-fact

Learjets are small passenger planes.

5 Draw in the pilots and the tail.

Nascar

1 Start with the body of the car.

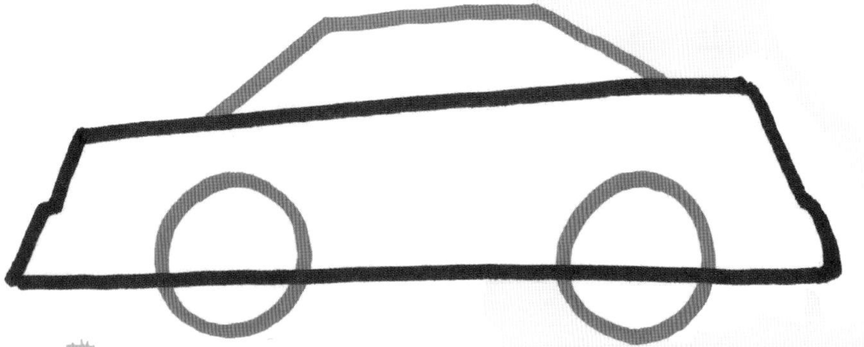

You can do it!

Use a felt-tip for the lines. Colour in with coloured felt-tips.

2 Add the roof and wheels.

3 Add the spoiler, lights, bumpers and hubcaps.

Splat-a fact

NASCAR stands for National Association for Stock Car Auto Racing.

4 Add the driver and all finishing details.

24

Electric train

MAKE SURE AN ADULT HELPS YOU WHEN USING SCISSORS!

1 Start by cutting out the main body of the train.

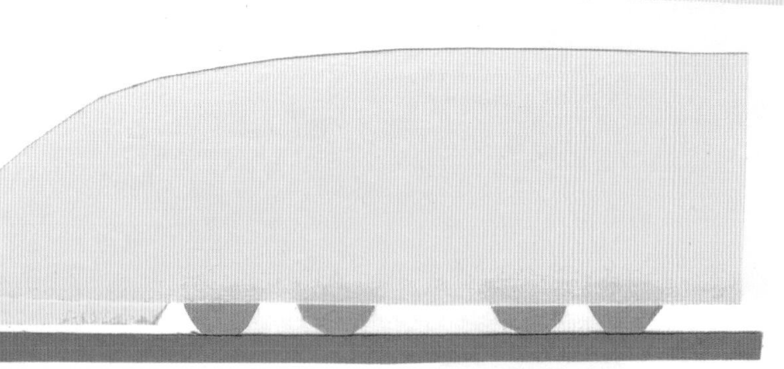

Splat-a-fact

The fastest trains are powered by electricity.

2 Cut out four wheels, the rail track and the nose part. Stick down.

Draw in the curly shell.

3 Cut out the windsceen, side panel and red stripe. Stick down.

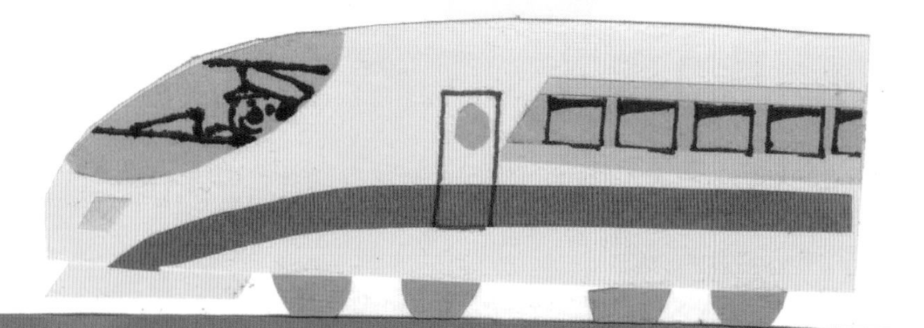

You can do it!

Cut out the shapes from coloured paper and glue in place. Use a felt-tip for details.

4 Cut out a light and windows then stick down. Draw in the driver and any other remaining details.

Spitfire

You can do it!

Use a pencil for the lines. Colour using watercolour washes.

1 Start with an oval for the Spitfire's fuselage and a circle for the propeller cap.

2 Draw in the cockpit and the pilot.

Splat-a-fact

The Spitfire was a British fighter aircraft from World War II.

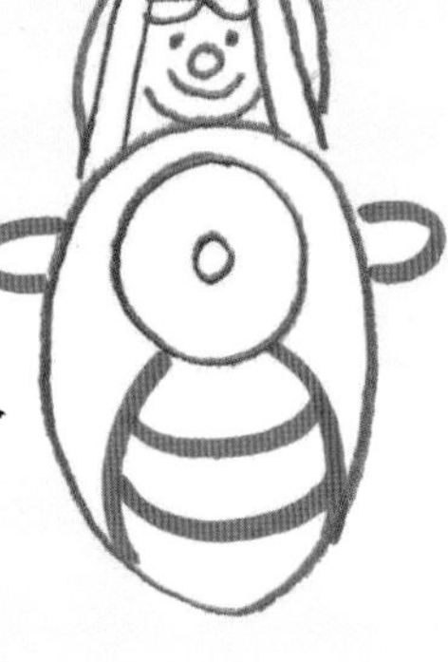

3 Draw in the engine parts.

4 Draw in the wings.

5 Draw in the horizontal and vertical stabilisers.

Beetle

1 Start by drawing the car's body and roof.

2 Draw in the rear wheel arches and the bumper.

Splat-a-fact
The beetle was one of the first rear-engined cars.

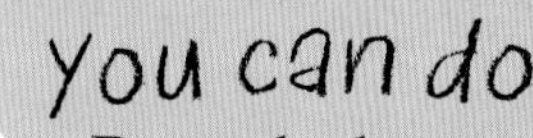

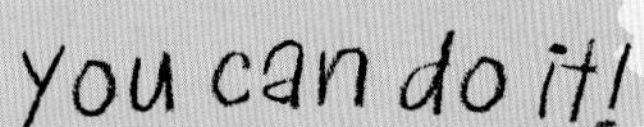

You can do it!
Draw the lines with a felt-tip and stick down torn tissue paper for colour.

3 Draw in the windows and the bonnet.

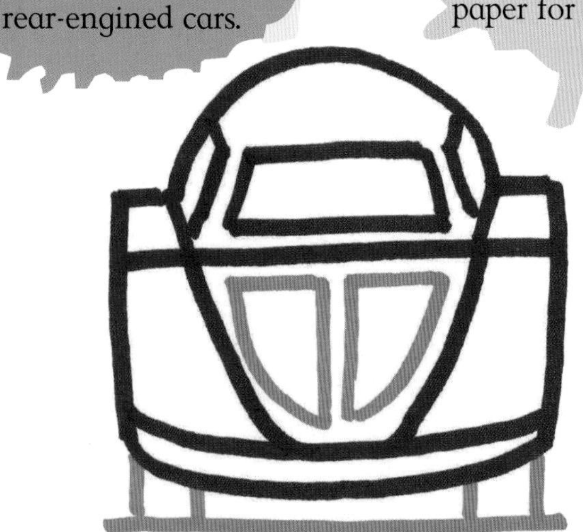

4 Add detail to the bonnet and draw in the wheels.

5 Add the headlights, wing mirrors and windsceen reflection.

Freight train

1 Start by drawing the main body of the train.

2 Draw in the undercarriage.

You can do it!
Use a felt-tip for the lines. Use coloured pencils. Place paper on a bumpy surface to add texture.

3 Add the windows and side panels.

Splat-a-fact
Freight trains carry goods over very long distances.

4 Draw in the headlight, horn and front grill. Add the driver.

Pitts special

1 Start by drawing the main shape of the plane.

Splat-a-fact

The Pitts special is an aerobatic biplane used for high speed stunts and racing.

2 Draw in the pilot, the horizontal stabiliser and a lightning flash.

3 Draw in the wings and add a propeller.

4 Draw in the undercarriage.

you can do it!

Use a felt-tip for the lines. Add colour with wax crayons using different kinds of scribbly marks to add variety. Paint over with a watercolour wash.

F1 car
1 Start by drawing the body and rear wing of the car.
2 Draw in the wheels, rear section and a line for the ground.
3 Draw in the front wing and the side and top engine air intakes.
4 Draw in wheel nuts and camera mount. Add the driver.
You can do it!
Use a felt-tip for the lines and add colour using coloured pencils.
Splat-a-fact
The first ever Formula One race was held in 1950.

1

Tank engine

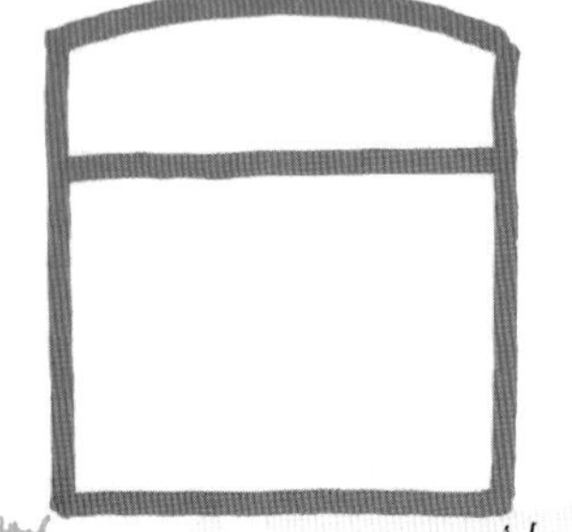

1 Start with the main body of the tank engine.

2 Draw in the roof, sides and undercarriage.

3 Draw in a chimney, boiler and windows.

Splat-a-fact

Tank engine are compact versions of steam locomotives.

4 Add the wheels, boiler, bumper and coupling details.

5 Draw in the tunnel, driver and rails. Add a puff of smoke from the chimney.

You can do it!

Use a felt-tip for the lines and add colour with watercolour paints. Use a sponge to dab on some colour for added texture.

Glider

1 Start with the glider's curved fuselage.

2 Draw in the cockpit and the pilot.

3 Draw in the vertical stabiliser and the undercarriage hatch.

You can do it!

Use a felt-tip for the lines and colour in with coloured pencils. Blend the pencils with your fingers.

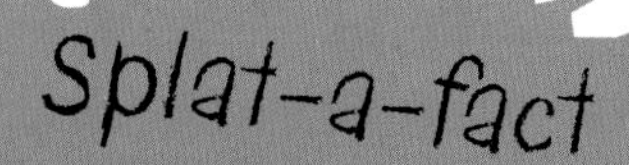

Splat-a-fact

Gliders have no engine. Thermals (hot air rising from the ground) carry gliders up through the air.

4 Add the wing, tail stripe, back light and to section of the vertical stabiliser.

Hot rod

Splat-a-fact
Hot rods are street racing cars built from old cars.

1 Start by drawing the car body.

2 Draw in the wheels, wheel arches and the ground.

You can do it!
Use a felt-tip for the lines and add colour using coloured ink washes.

3 Draw in the windows, and the bumpers. Add the driver.

4 Add the headlights, big engine and flame decoration.

Index